SPACE!

THE STARS

GAIL MACK

Marshall Cavendish Benchmark
99 White Plains Road
Tarrytown, New York 10591-9001
www.marshallcavendish.us
Text copyright © 2010 by Marshall Cavendish Corporation

Editor: Karen Ang
Publisher: Michelle Bisson
Art Director: Anahid Hamparian
Series design by Daniel Roode
Production by nSight Inc

Library of Congress Cataloging-in-Publication Data

Mack, Gail.
  The stars / by Gail Mack.
     p. cm. -- (Space!)
  Summary: "Describes the stars, including their history, their composition, and their
roles in the solar system"--Provided by publisher.
  Includes bibliographical references and index.
  ISBN 978-0-7614-4250-9
  1. Stars--Juvenile literature. 2. Galaxies--Juvenile literature. I.
Title.
  QB801.7.M32 2010
  523.8--dc22
2009014655

Front cover: An image from the Hubble Space Telescope shows a portion of a nebula
where stars are being born.
Title page: An image of the Egg Nebula
Cover Photo: NASA-ESA / AP Images
Photo research by Candlepants Incorporated

The photographs in this book are used by permission and through the courtesy of:
Super Stock: Pixtal, 1, 9; Digital Vision Ltd., 6, 12, 33. NASA: Babak Tafreshi, 4, 5; 15, 26,
30, 43; J PL-Caltech/T. Velusamy, 17; Jim Misti & Steve Mazlin, 19; JPL/Caltech/R. Hurt, 22;
J PL-Caltech/R. Hurt (SSC), 23, 37; L.Barranger(STScI)JPL/Caltech/R. Gehrz (University
of Minnesota), 28; CXC/M. Weiss, 31; ESA/S. Beckwith (STScI)/HUDF Team, 34, 35; Hubble
Space Telescope Center, 39;. AP Images: NASA-ESA, 36; NASA, 41. Photo Researchers Inc.:
Baback Tafreshi, 38; Mike Agliolo, 44; Herman Eisenbeiss, 46; Gerard Lodriguss, 50. The
Image Works: SSPL, 48, 49. Getty Images: Stattmayer, 52. Marshall Cavendish Corporation:
51, 54.

Printed in Malaysia
123456

CONTENTS

1

WHAT IS A STAR?

Thousands of years ago in ancient Egypt, farmers watched for the brightest of all the stars to rise. The ancient Egyptians called the star Sothis, Bringer of the Nile Floods. Today we know it as Sirius, the Dog Star—brighter, larger, and hotter than the Sun. The name Sirius comes from a Greek word that means "scorching," or "sparkling." During the hot summer months of July, August, and September, Sirius rose at the same time as the Sun, and people believed that the star added its own heat to the Sun, making the summer days very hot.

The farmers used the rising of Sirius to plan their lives—to them the star was a sign each year that the Nile River would soon flood their lands. After the flood, they could plant their crops in the rich, moist earth. The ancient Egyptians also discovered

Stars twinkle above the Alborz Mountains in Iran. Sirius, the Dog Star, is the brightest star in the night sky.

that Sirius rose with the Sun not every 365 days—their calendar year—but every 365.25 days, which they thought made their year a little longer. In the year 46 BCE, the Roman emperor Julius Caesar corrected the calendar. Called the Julian calendar, the new calendar had three 365-day years, followed by a year with 366 days. Today we call this 366-day year a leap year and add an extra day to February, making the month twenty-nine days long instead of twenty-eight days.

In those ancient days, an **astronomer**—a scientist who studies stars and other **celestial** objects—named Ptolemy lived in Egypt. He observed stars like Sirius and **constellations**, which are groups of stars that together form patterns, shapes, or images in the sky. Ptolemy wondered about what he saw and what it could mean.

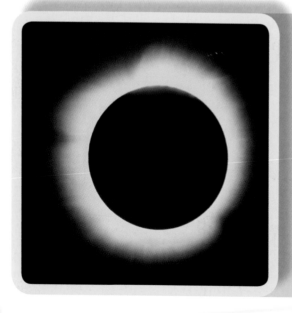

Throughout history, people have been observing the activities of the stars in the sky. One of the most recognizable star events is a solar eclipse. This occurs when the Moon moves between Earth and the Sun, and blocks most of the Sun.

ASTROLOGY

Many ancient people believed in astrology, which involves using the positions of the stars and planets to make predictions about future events. Emperors and other rulers had court astrologers who worked on their horoscopes, which were charts and pictures of the positions of the Sun, Moon, planets, and stars at the times the rulers were born. Some rulers used astrology to claim that the stars showed they were born to rule. Others used it to get rid of their enemies.

In ancient Greece, people also saw constellations and named them based on myths about their gods, heroes, and animals. During the Han Dynasty (from 206 BCE to 220 CE) the Chinese people grouped constellations by the four directions—East (Dragon), West (Tiger), North (Tortoise), and South (Scarlet Bird). The Tewa, who were early North American Pueblo people, identified a constellation they called Long Sash. They believed that Long Sash was a hero who led their people away from enemies, finding a new home for them in a star pattern in the sky that they called the "Endless Trail." (At the time, the Tewa did not know that the Endless Trail was actually a visible part of our galaxy called the Milky Way.) Thousands of years ago the ancient people of Central and South America also named the objects in the sky. The Maya, for example, called the Milky Way the World Tree, which was represented by a beautiful flowering tree called the Ceiba.

The ancient Romans also saw pictures in the constellations and named them. Roman warriors and emperors looked to the stars to predict whether they would win or lose important battles. They also observed the stars to predict their own fates.

NAVIGATING BY THE STARS

Early people in many other parts of the world braved the uncharted, unmarked oceans. By day, they navigated by the Sun—which is a star—and by night, they looked to the twinkling stars in the sky. The ancient Phoenicians sailed from the shores of their Middle Eastern lands, known today as Lebanon. The Phoenicians knew that at certain times of the year, at any one point on the globe, the Sun and stars would be at certain fixed distances above the horizon. During the day, they used the Sun's position to guide them east or west. At night, they held their fingers up to the sky to measure the stars' positions above the horizon.

Ancient Chinese and Greek sailors also used constellations as their guides. More than two thousand years ago, the Maori from the Polynesian island we now know as New Zealand explored the Pacific Ocean, also navigating by the stars. Like others, they created myths around the star patterns they used.

Powerful telescopes and satellites allow scientists to examine celestial objects, such as the star clusters in the Tarantula Nebula.

Modern astronomers use powerful telescopes on the ground and special equipment on **satellites** in space to see the stars. Their telescopes show us spectacular close-up pictures of stars that are close to Earth or very far away. Using this equipment, scientists can see new stars being born, and old, dying stars exploding like giant fireworks. Astronomers all over the world also use computers and other kinds of electronic instruments to figure out what the stars are made of and how big, how old, and how far from Earth they are. But most nights we can use our unaided eyes to see the twinkling stars in the sky.

TWINKLE, TWINKLE, LITTLE STAR

On a clear, dark night, it is possible to see about six thousand different stars shining in the sky. When we look at the star, it seems to twinkle. This is because in space, a star sends out, or radiates, its light as straight rays. But when rays of starlight enter Earth's atmosphere, the movement of air changes the light as the rays travel down through the atmosphere to the ground. Some light rays come straight to us, and others bend in different directions. This bending makes the starlight look like it is flickering or twinkling.

DEFINING AND CLASSIFYING A STAR

A star is a huge, glowing ball of hot gases—mostly hydrogen, helium, and a hot, gas-like substance called **plasma**. Many other chemical elements, like calcium, nitrogen, or carbon, may also be present. These gases and elements stay with the star and do not float off into space because of **gravity**. The star's gravity pulls the gases and elements down toward the star's center.

Astronomers look at several different characteristics in order to classify stars. One characteristic is a star's **luminosity**, or the rate at which it radiates light energy. Luminosity depends on the star's size, radius (the distance from the star's center to its surface), mass (the amount and weight of material the star contains), surface temperature, and its distance from Earth.

Luminosity

Astronomers describe a star's luminosity by using a system of **magnitude,** which was originally created by an ancient scientist named Hipparchus. Hipparchus's system of magnitude numbered groups of stars according to how bright they looked to us from Earth. He called the brightest ones first-magnitude stars. The next brightest were second-magnitude stars, and the next, third-magnitude stars, right down to the faintest points of light he could see—the sixth-magnitude stars. A star of the first magnitude is about two-and-a-half times as bright as a star of the second magnitude. That star is two-and-a-half times as bright as a star of the third magnitude, and so on. A first magnitude star is one hundred times as bright as one of the sixth magnitude.

Today's astronomers still use Hipparchus's system, but they have expanded it to classify many more stars that have been discovered using strong telescopes. Today there are two different kinds of magnitude. Visual magnitude is the brightness of a star as we see it from Earth. Absolute magnitude tells us how bright stars would appear to be if they were all the same distance—32.6 **light-years**—from Earth.

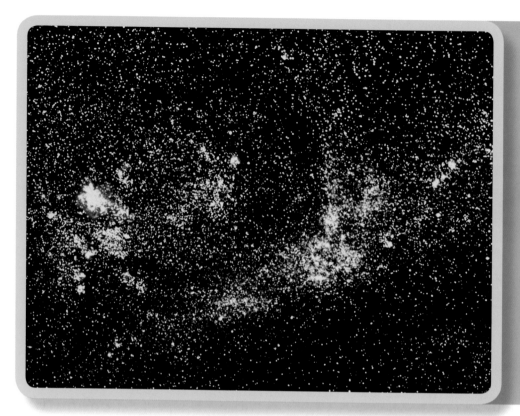

Without visual and absolute magnitudes, it would be difficult to determine which stars are truly brighter than others. This is especially true when there are many stars close together, such as in this galaxy called the Large Magellanic Cloud.

Two stars seen from Earth could appear to have the same visual magnitudes even if their sizes, temperatures, and distances from Earth are different. One star could be larger and hotter, but farther away than the other, while the other star could be smaller and cooler, but closer to our planet. So both could appear to be equally bright. But the same two stars would have different absolute magnitudes because they are really at different distances from Earth. Astronomers use telescopes, computers, and mathematical calculations to figure out stars' distances from Earth.

HOW FAR AWAY ARE THE STARS?

At 93 million miles (150 million kilometers) away, the Sun is Earth's closest star. But other stars are so far away that using miles or meters or kilometers to measure their distances from Earth does not work. For example, the closest star to Earth besides the Sun is Proxima Centauri, and it is about 24 trillion miles (39 trillion km) away. So astronomers came up with a unit—called a light-year—to measure really long distances in space. Light travels at 186,322.324 miles (299,792,458 km) per second. In one year, light travels 5.89 trillion miles (9.46 trillion km). Scientists figured that using the speed of light in a year would help to give accurate measurements.

LIGHT-TRAVEL TIME	MILES	KM
1 light-second	186,322.324	299.8 million
1 light-minute	11.18 million	17.98 million
1 light-hour	670.76 million	1.08 billion
1 light-day	16.098 billion	25.9 billion
1 light-week	112.69 billion	181.3 billion
1 light-month (30 days)	482.95 billion	777.06 billion
1 light-year	5.89 trillion	9.46 trillion

Parsecs and Parallax

Another useful unit, called a parsec, measures super-long distances in space. One parsec equals 3.26 light-years, or 19.2 trillion miles (30.9 trillion km). The distance that astronomers use to measure absolute magnitude—32.6 light-years—is equal to 10 parsecs. The word *parsec* combines two words—*parallax* and *second*. A second is a unit in the metric system used to measure both time (there are 60 seconds in a minute) and angles. Angles are divided into degrees, minutes, and seconds. Seconds are used only to measure extremely long distances. Astronomers use seconds, as do sailors, pilots, and others who need to find longitudes and latitudes.

Astronomers use parallax to measure the distance from Earth to a star by calculating measurements for a triangle. The triangle is formed by drawing imaginary lines from points in Earth's orbit around the Sun to nearby stars. Scientists then use math to calculate the triangle's measurements. These parallax calculations give astronomers the star's distance from Earth. However, measuring distances by parallax works only for stars that are up to 400 light-years away from Earth.

Brightness

For stars farther away, astronomers use brightness and color to measure distances from Earth. When they know the star's brightness and its distance from Earth, they can use mathematics to calculate its luminosity. Large stars are brighter because they send out more energy than smaller stars. The light of a star that is far from Earth is dimmer than the light from a closer star, even if the faraway star is hotter and larger.

Using today's powerful telescopes, astronomers have discovered stars brighter than Hipparchus could ever have imagined. There are stars that are brighter than first magnitude and fainter than sixth magnitude. Stars brighter than first need magnitude numbers lower than 1. For example, Rigel, in the Orion constellation, has a visual magnitude of 0.12. Very, very bright stars have negative magnitudes. Sirius, the brightest star we can see from Earth, has a visual magnitude of -1.46. Canopus, the second-brightest star in the sky has a visual magnitude of -0.72. But

Canopus is the second-brightest star in the sky, but because it is located in the Southern Hemisphere, it cannot be seen from most of North America and nearly all of Europe.

our Sun wins—its visual magnitude is a whopping -26.72. Even though it is technically not the brightest star in the sky, because it is the one closest to our planet, it appears to be brighter.

People who study the night sky with a telescope can measure a star's brightness with a photometer. A photometer is a device that uses a pointer to show the strength of a star's light. Photometers may be part of a telescope or held separately. When light falls on a photometer's sensor, an electric current moves the pointer.

Color and Surface Temperature

Some stars are extremely hot, while others are very cool. The clue to a star's surface temperature is its color. The hottest stars are white or sometimes blue. Cooler stars are red. A yellow star is hotter than a red star, but cooler than a white one. Astronomers can tell by the intensity of a star's color how hot, cool, or cold it is. They use a unit of measurment called the **kelvin** (K) to measure the surface temperatures of stars. Scientists use letters of the alphabet to classify stars by color and surface temperature. There are seven major kinds of stars.

Although a star looks as though it has only one color (usually white), it actually radiates the whole range of colors that you see in a rainbow—red, orange, yellow, green, blue, indigo, and violet. The colors in a star also tell scientists what elements are in the star. The colors make up the visible light spectrum. Scientists

This image taken by the NASA Spitzer Space Telescope shows a young star (center, white) blowing "bubbles" of gas and dust. The bubbles are shown in blue and green, which tells scientists that they are made of hydrogen gas and dust particles in space.

STAR TYPES	COLOR	APPROXIMATE SURFACE TEMPERATURE IN KELVINS (K)
O	Blue	More than 25,000 K
B	Blue	11,000 – 25,000 K
A	Blue	7,500 – 11,000 K
F	Blue to White	6,000 – 7,500 K
G	White to Yellow	5,000 – 6,000 K
K	Orange to Red	3,500 – 5,000 K
M	Red	Under 3,500 K

study a star's visible light spectrum with an instrument called a spectrograph. The colors they see identify the chemical gases that make up the star.

Temperature

Scientists today may use three different temperature scales—Fahrenheit, Celsius, and Kelvin. Each has a different set of divisions that show degrees. The divisions are based on different starting points for zero degrees. The Fahrenheit scale is used mostly in the United States. Most other countries and scientists use the Celsius, or Centigrade, scale. Scientists who

Stars of different ages and sizes can be found near each other. As they age and undergo changes, they release or absorb different materials in space, shown here as blue, pink, and orange clouds.

need to measure very low temperatures prefer the Kelvin scale. Degrees in this scale are called kelvins (K).

Scientists can rank the heat of stars based on the temperatures in kelvins. For example, Betelgeuse is a cool star because its surface temperature is only 3500 K. It emits more red and orange light. Rigel is a hot star because its temperature is 15,000 K, and it is blue.

SIZE

Stars come in many sizes. They range from tiny neutron stars—with a radius of just 6 miles (9.66 km)—to **dwarf** stars the size of Earth, which has a radius of about 3,961 miles (6,378 km), to giant and supergiant stars that are several times larger.

The Sun's radius—the distance from its center to its surface—is about 430,000 miles (695,500 km). That may seem large to us, but to astronomers, it makes the Sun a yellow dwarf star. Astronomers use the radius of the Sun as a unit of length when they measure the size of other stars. The Sun's radius is called the **solar** radius. If a star has a radius that is more than one time larger than the Sun's, it is measured in solar radii, which is the plural for radius. For example, Alpha Centauri A, the third-closest star to Earth, has a radius of 1.05 solar radii. With a radius just slightly bigger than the Sun's, it is almost the same size. Rigel is much bigger—it measures 78 solar radii. That means its radius is 78 times that of the Sun. Antares, the brightest star in the constellation Scorpius—and among the brightest in the sky—is enormous. Its size is about 700 solar radii.

MASS

Just as they use the Sun's radius to express the sizes of stars, astronomers use the Sun's mass—called the solar mass—to describe the masses of stars. Mass is the amount of matter, or material, in an object. The mass of the Sun is 2×10^{27} tons. If you wrote out that number, you would write 2 followed by twenty-seven zeros! Alpha Centauri A's mass is 1.08 solar masses, while Rigel's mass is 17 solar masses.

Even though stars may be about the same size, they may have different densities. Density is the mass of a star. The more tightly packed the mass in a star is, the denser it is. Density determines how heavy or light an object is for its size. For example, the Sun's density is about 90 pounds per cubic foot (1.4 grams per cubic centimeter). That is 1.4 times the density of water and less than one-third of Earth's average density. Neutron stars are the tiniest and densest stars we know of. Neutron stars are only about 15 miles (24 km) across, but their mass can be between 1.4 and 3 times that of the Sun.

2

THE BIRTH AND DEATH OF STARS

Stars have life cycles. New stars are always forming, growing, changing, and—after billions of years—destroying themselves. Many are born in the swirling nebulae—clouds of gases and dust—of our home galaxy, the Milky Way. The life of a star begins when a very dense area in a nebula collapses inward into a ball and starts to shrink. Its own gravity pulls the gas and other elements in the cloud together to form an embryo star called a protostar. The protostar's outer shell forms a spinning disk. It takes about one hundred thousand years for the protostar to form. When it does, its surface temperature is about 4000 K.

An illustration provided by NASA shows the birth of a star.

As the protostar shrinks, it spins faster and the temperature in its core keeps rising. Finally, it gets so hot that nuclear burning, or fusion, begins. At that point, the temperature is about 15 million K, or 27 million degrees Fahrenheit (15 million degrees C). The shrinking slows as the "baby star" becomes an adult. It begins generating its own light and heat as a result of the nuclear fusion. It then becomes a variable star. Like a flickering lightbulb, the brightness of this star varies.

AN AGING STAR

As the star ages, it is still contracting, or shrinking. It continues to do this for millions or billions of years. Finally, when the pressure from the **radiation** inside is balanced with its gravity, the star stops contracting. This is what astronomers call a main sequence star.

This main sequence star is fusing hydrogen **atoms** together to make helium atoms. Because stars have only so much hydrogen in their cores, or centers, their lives as main sequence stars are limited. A star's main sequence lifetime depends on its average luminosity, how much of its mass it uses for nuclear fusion, and how fast it uses up its hydrogen. Stars spend nearly all of their lives—about 90 percent—on the main sequence.

The larger a star's mass, the less time it will spend on the main sequence. The rate of fusion is extremely sensitive to temperature, and fusion happens much faster in stars with large masses and very hot cores.

The Sun is a main sequence star, and we are lucky that the Sun is not more massive than it is because high-mass stars exhaust their hydrogen very quickly. The Sun will spend about 10 billion years on the main sequence. Since it is about 4.5 billion years old right now, it is halfway through its main sequence lifetime. The Sun's time on the main sequence will end when it has converted most of its hydrogen into helium and its core becomes too cool to use the helium.

What happens when a star like the Sun runs out of the hydrogen in its core? Once a star's heat source at the core is gone and the core cools, it begins to contract and become smaller and denser. As the star continues to contract, the core and the shell around it—which contains hydrogen—begin to heat up again. In the shell around its core, the star fuses hydrogen into helium even faster than before. The shell expands and moves farther and farther away from the core and grows cooler. The star's light begins to change color. (In the case of a Sun-like star it turns from a yellow dwarf into a red giant.) Its core heats up again until the nuclei, or centers, of the helium atoms begin to fuse into the nuclei of carbon and oxygen atoms.

At the last stage of the star's life, its core has become so hot and its force of gravity so weak that its outer layers blow away in the stellar winds. Its shell turns into dust. Eventually, all the

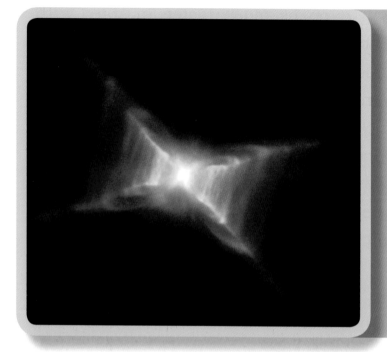

The star in the center is called HD 44179, and it is dying. Scientists have given it the nickname the Red Rectangle because of the pattern it is creating as it ejects its outer layers and forms a nebula.

dust will blow away and only the star's hot core will remain. The fusion has stopped, so now the core is made mostly of carbon and oxygen and its temperature is about 100,000 K. With no more fuel to burn, the star gets cooler and cooler, fainter and fainter, until it is impossible to see. Its life cycle has ended.

Billions of years from now, the Sun will become a red giant. Many astronomers believe it will expand so much that its atmosphere will surround the Earth, destroying the planet. However, others believe it is possible that the Sun will lose much of its mass and gravity. If that happens, Earth and the other planets will no longer be attracted to the Sun and will move away from it. Billions of years later, the Sun will run out of all its fuel and become a white dwarf star and then a black dwarf. At that point it will only be a small, dim reminder of its former blazing glory.

WHITE DWARFS

A white dwarf is a star that has come to the end of its life. It has run out of fuel and has a dense core made of carbon and oxygen. The core of a white dwarf is so dense that if it were the size of a ping-pong ball, it would weigh as much as an SUV! A white dwarf may not be white. The first few that were discovered were white, but now scientists know that their color depends on their temperatures. The hottest white dwarfs are violet, while the coolest are deep red. They radiate only a tiny bit of light, so we cannot see them without a telescope. Eventually, white dwarfs become cold, black dwarfs.

HIGH-MASS STARS AND SUPERNOVAS

The deaths of high-mass stars are far more spectacular than those of stars with lower masses, like the Sun. Scientists call the deaths of these high-mass stars Type II supernovas.

When a star that has ten times more mass than the Sun uses up the helium in its core, it burns and changes other elements.

For example, it might change carbon into iron. But iron does not radiate heat or light, even if it is burned into another element. With no radiation pressure to resist the force of gravity, the iron core collapses and the star's outer layers are crushed into a hard, fast-spinning core. Matter stops being pulled into the core, causing a Type II supernova explosion. The explosion suddenly releases an enormous amount of energy.

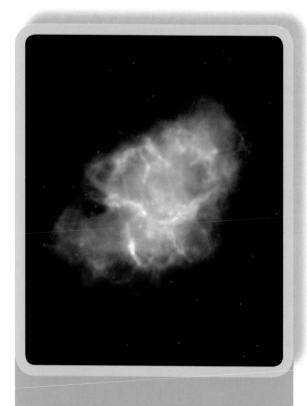

The Crab Nebula is the remains of an exploded supernova.

Some supernovas burn more brightly than a galaxy of a billion stars, and some can be seen during daytime. About five hundred years ago, Chinese astronomers recorded observations of a supernova they saw during the day. Today we still see evidence of that ancient explosion—it left behind a huge gas and dust cloud called the Crab Nebula.

Supernova explosions shoot many elements into **interstellar space**. Supernovas are very important because they produce most of the gases that will find their way into stars and planets of the future. Our own planet and everything on it is made of elements that came from a supernova explosion. Without the fiery deaths of massive stars, there would be no oxygen, carbon, or other elements that make life on Earth possible.

NEUTRON STARS AND PULSARS

Scientists predicted the existence of neutron stars in 1938. A neutron star is the smallest and densest star known. Neutron stars have a diameter of about 15 miles (24 km) across, but their masses are about one to three times that of the Sun. A neutron star starts out as a large star—at least ten times as large as the Sun—and eventually runs out of hydrogen to burn. With no radiation to resist its strong force of gravity, it collapses and becomes a neutron star.

A neutron star is tiny, but unbelievably powerful. Its intense gravitational and magnetic fields would pull an approaching spacecraft to pieces. A neutron star spins at high speed and has a magnetic field billions of times stronger than the most powerful magnets on Earth. Its magnetic field can generate electric voltages 30 million times more powerful than lightning bolts. The magnetic field rotates with the star, which can result in dangerous storms of high-energy particles being torn from

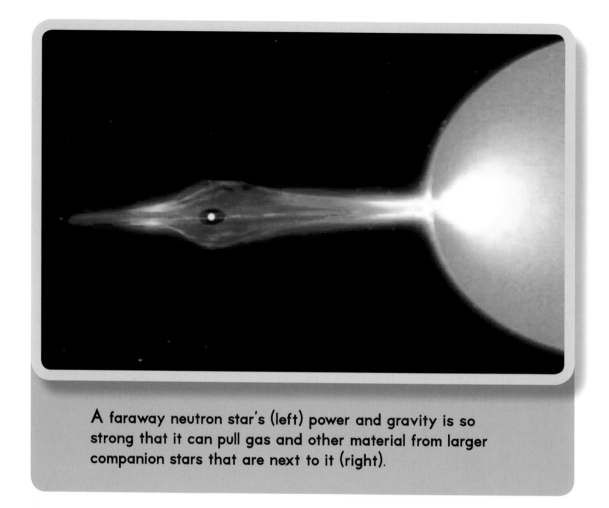

A faraway neutron star's (left) power and gravity is so strong that it can pull gas and other material from larger companion stars that are next to it (right).

the star's surface. These high-energy particles produce a thin beam of radio waves that rotates with the star.

Scientists have observed what they call pulsing radiation, or pulsars, which act like the revolving light of a lighthouse. They believe that the pulsars are actually fast-spinning neutron stars. Astronomers discovered the first pulsar in 1967. Since then, they have found about a thousand pulsars.

BLACK HOLES

Black holes are born from supernovas. Black holes come in different sizes, and their forces of gravity are so powerful that not even light can escape. That is why we cannot see black holes—not even with a telescope. There is no real surface to measure, only a region and a kind of boundary around the black hole. This boundary is called the event horizon. No one can see beyond the boundary, but scientists are sure black holes exist because matter that is near them behaves in odd ways. Gases near a black hole, for example, zip around it at nearly the speed of light and emit high-energy radiation. Black holes are not really empty. They hold what is left of stars that have

A NASA illustration reveals what a black hole most likely looks like as it spins and draws in material and objects in space.

exploded in supernovas. The star has been so compressed that it has zero volume and infinite, or unlimited, density. It is called a **singularity**. Our Sun can never become a black hole because its mass is too small. A star must have about ten times the mass of the Sun to become a black hole.

Astronomers believe that most galaxies—including the Milky Way—contain supermassive black holes at their centers. Through observations of the high-speed orbits of stars and gases at the centers of galaxies, scientists have found gigantic black holes that each have the mass of a billion Suns. They are not sure how such enormous black holes are created. Could it be that one black hole forms and gulps up huge amounts of matter over millions of years? Could a cluster of starlike black holes form and then become one? Or could it be that a single monstrous gas cloud collapses and forms a supermassive black hole? They hope that more observations and discoveries will yield the answer.

QUASARS

Quasars are connected to supermassive black holes. A quasar's power depends on the mass of its central supermassive black hole and the rate at which the black hole swallows up matter. A quasar forms when large quantities of gas are pulled into the black hole so fast that the energy produced is a thousand times greater than the galaxy itself.

Quasars are tiny regions with diameters that are about one-millionth the diameter of their host galaxies. But one quasar radiates as much energy as a thousand or more galaxies. Quasars are the most powerful sources of X rays, a type of radiation, discovered so far. Quasars are also intense sources of visible light. Some quasars are so bright that they can be seen from 12 billion light-years away.

This image of Einstein's Cross appears to have five different quasars grouped together, but there is really only quasar. Light is being bent by nearby galaxies, causing the image to be magnified and duplicated. Quasars like these are called lensed quasars.

3

GALAXIES

A galaxy is a collection of billions of celestial objects and stars and clouds of gases and dust. The stars and everything else in the galaxy are held together by their gravitational pull. A galaxy's mass is much larger than that of its stars or any other objects. Astronomers think that galaxies also contain enormous amounts of an invisible material called dark matter. The dark matter does not send out any kind of electromagnetic energy, but its gravitational pull on visible objects nearby makes scientists believe that it exists in the huge distances between the stars.

Astronomers can see far-distant galaxies because of the starlight that shines from so many stars. Galaxies are classified based on a system devised by the astronomer Edwin Hubble. There are three types of galaxies—spiral, elliptical, and irregular galaxies. Our own Milky Way is a spiral galaxy.

In 2004, the Hubble Space Telescope obtained this view of nearly 10,000 galaxies.

There are other galaxies with different shapes. Some are called peculiar galaxies. These have unusual shapes, perhaps made by a collision of two galaxies. Others are called starburst galaxies. In these, many stars form very quickly over 10 million years, which is about a month in the life of a 10-billion-year-old galaxy. Some galaxies are called active galaxies. These send out enormous amounts of radiation from their cores. They can emit this radiation for millions of years. Spiral, elliptical, and irregular galaxies can all be active galaxies.

This ring of dark matter is about 2.6 million light-years across and was found in a galaxy about 5 billion light-years away from Earth.

THE MILKY WAY

The Milky Way is the galaxy that is home to our Solar System and billions of stars. It is about 100,000 light-years across and is shaped like a thin disk with a bulge in the center. The bulge is a thick bar of older white stars that stretches for about 15,000 light-years, or 5.88 trillion miles (9.46 trillion km) across the middle of the galaxy. Stars, dust, and gas are sprinkled throughout the galaxy in long, spiral arms. Because of its shape, astronomers classify the Milky Way as a spiral galaxy. The Milky Way is so huge that about ten smaller galaxies orbit around it as if it were a planet.

The Milky Way is also the name of a part of our galaxy that can be seen by the eye alone, without the help of telescopes. The Milky Way stretches across the dark sky like a wide ribbon of starlight. If we were flying in a spacecraft far above the Milky Way and looked down at it, our galaxy would look like a pinwheel. From inside it, we see only hazy light from nearby stars because interstellar dust blocks the starlight. All the billions of stars in the Milky Way are bound together by gravitational force. Our Sun is one of those billions of stars and is 24,000 light-years from the center of the galaxy.

An illustration of the Milky Way galaxy as it would appear from above. As the illustration shows, the Sun (and our Solar System) is just one small part of this enormous galaxy.

An astronomer uses a telescope to look at the visible part of the Milky Way.

OTHER GALAXIES

In the 1920s, astronomer Edwin Hubble discovered that there are many other galaxies beyond our own in the **universe**. In fact, there are trillions of galaxies, each with hundreds of thousands to billions and trillions of stars. Some galaxies may have small diameters of just a few thousand light-years, while others are millions of light-years across.

The Milky Way is part of a small cluster of about thirty-six galaxies called the Local Group. In turn, the Local Group is part of a supercluster of galaxies called the Virgo Supercluster, which contains a few thousand galaxies.

One of our nearest neighbors is the Andromeda galaxy, also called M31. It has about 300 billion stars and is about 2.5 million light-years away. Like the Milky Way, it has a central bulge.

Galaxies that are near each other may interact or even collide. The two spiral galaxies shown here are so close that they are distorting and disrupting each other. Scientists predict that in a few billion years, these two galaxies will join together to form a much larger one.

Astronomers think the bulge contains a black hole. Andromeda is traveling toward the Milky Way at about 186 miles (299.27 km) per second. In about 2 billion years they might collide.

Galaxies sometimes do collide, with spectacular results. For example, the Cartwheel galaxy—500 million light-years from Earth—collided with another galaxy and formed two rings of gas and brand-new stars. The Whirlpool galaxy has a spiral shape, thanks to a small galaxy near it. The little galaxy brushes against the larger Whirlpool galaxy, and the small galaxy's gravity may be pulling at the larger one, shaping it into a spiral.

The discovery of galaxies beyond the Milky Way meant that the universe was much larger than scientists had thought. Edwin Hubble had developed the system for classifying galaxies and discovered that the faraway galaxies were moving away from each other faster and faster. This relationship between speed and distance is known as Hubble's Law. This law proves that the universe is expanding. The greater the distance between two galaxies, the faster they are moving away from each other.

The Magellanic Clouds

Two other neighbors orbit our galaxy. These are the Magellanic Clouds, which are types of galaxies named after the Portuguese explorer Ferdinand Magellan, who saw them in 1519 during his first voyage around the world. The Clouds are much smaller than

A Hubble Space Telescope image of the Small Magellanic Cloud shows many embryonic, or infant, stars just starting to develop.

the Milky Way. The Large Magellanic Cloud (LMC), is the closest to our galaxy—about 160,000 light-years away—and it contains 15 billion stars. The Small Magellanic Cloud (SMC) is about 180,000 light-years away and contains only around 5 billion stars.

OUR SOLAR SYSTEM

Within the Milky Way are an unimaginable number of celestial objects. Our Solar System is just one of many systems that exist throughout the universe, but it is the most important one to us. The Solar System is heliocentric, which means the Sun is at the center and all other things revolve around it. After the Sun formed, rings of material—including gases, particles, dust, and rocks—circled the new star. As these things crashed into each other, they began to form celestial bodies, like planets, moons, asteroids, and meteorites. The Sun's gravity causes the planets and other celestial objects to orbit around it.

Eventually, the Solar System was established. None of the planets in the Solar System are exactly alike. They have different sizes, colors, and chemical compositions. Some have many moons, while others have few or none. Some planets even have rings.

Many planetary characteristics are the result of the Sun's influence. The star's gravity, solar winds, magnetic forces, heat, and light all affected how the planets were created or shaped. In

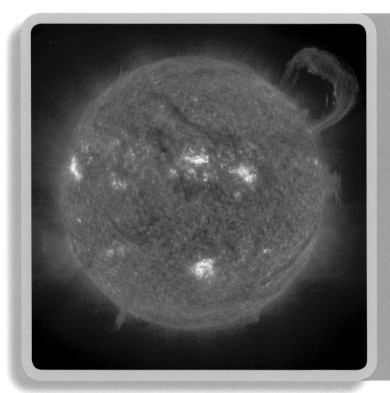

Like most stars, the Sun is a pulsing mass of hot gas and other materials. Holes in parts of the surface of the Sun allow gases and particles to escape. This solar wind travels throughout our Solar System, affecting, and sometimes damaging, planets and other celestial bodies.

Earth's case, the planet's proximity to and resources from the Sun enabled life to develop and survive. Without the Sun, there would be no Solar System. And we, as humans, owe everything to this life-giving star.

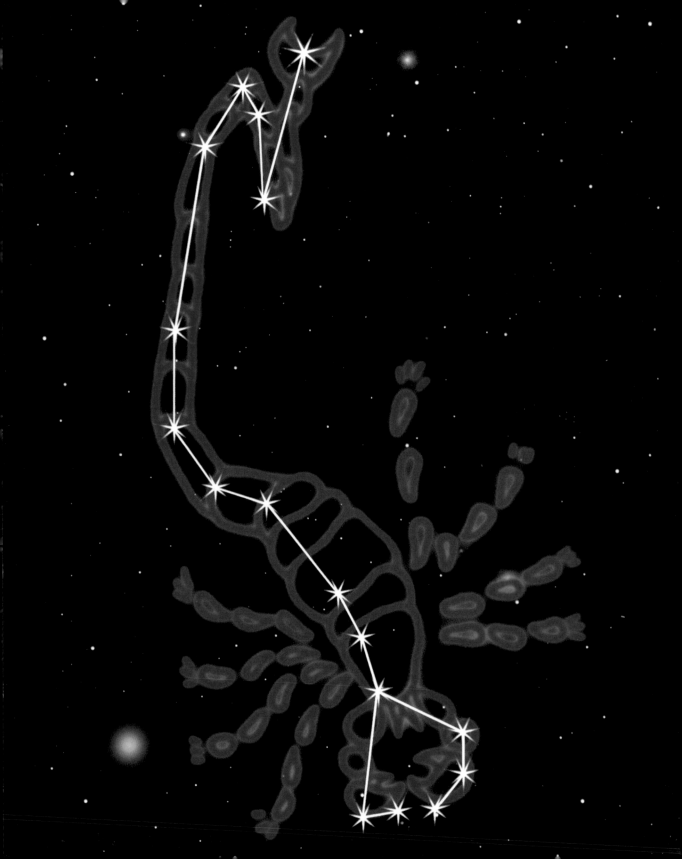

4
STARGAZING

housands of years ago, early people saw that every year the seasons changed when certain constellations moved to different positions in the sky. These people may have named these constellations after animals, mythical creatures and heroes, and other objects. They drew pictures on star maps that connected the stars and helped them remember each constellation. Today we use the constellations to track stars and artificial satellites and to help astronomers and navigators find certain stars.

THE CELESTIAL SPHERE

To better visualize and understand constellations, astronomers use the celestial sphere. This is a gigantic, imaginary ball that surrounds Earth. All the stars and planets seem to be attached

A computer illustration shows some of the stars that make up the Scorpius constellation.

to the inside surface of this sphere. To make it easier to find objects on the sphere, astronomers placed imaginary north and south poles and a celestial equator on the sphere. The celestial poles and equator are above Earth's North and South Poles and its equator. Depending on where we are, when we look up at the sky we see only half of the celestial sphere—either the northern half, or hemisphere, above the celestial equator, or the southern hemisphere, below it. (The celestial hemispheres line up with Earth's Northern and Southern Hemispheres.)

As they are observed from season to season, the constellations appear to be changing position around the celestial poles. This is because Earth is moving—it is spinning on its **axis** and rotating around the Sun. Polaris, the pole star, is located at the end of

Special photography can reveal star trails, which are the apparent paths the stars take as they revolve around the North Pole, or in this case, the North Star Polaris.

the "handle" of the constellation known as the Little Dipper. This bright star is called the North Star because it is almost exactly over the North Pole. The sky seems to rotate around Polaris. Polaris is often used for navigation in the Northern Hemisphere because it always indicates north. However, because stars are always moving and changing, Polaris will not always be so close to the North Pole. Scientists predict that in a few thousand years, a different star will become the North Star.

As Earth rotates around the Sun, it looks to us like the Sun is also moving around the celestial sphere, along a path called the ecliptic. The ecliptic is the circular path the Sun travels along among the constellations during one year. The changing positions of the Sun and the constellations are the result of Earth's movements and where, exactly, you are standing on Earth when you look at them. Twice a year, in spring and in fall, the ecliptic crosses the celestial equator at opposite sides. These crossings also mark the spring and fall equinoxes. The equinoxes are the two dates (around March 21 and September 23) when the Sun crosses Earth's equator. On those dates, day and night are of equal length all over the world.

The Zodiac

The zodiac is an imaginary belt on the celestial sphere. The zodiac is divided into twelve equal parts, each named for a different constellation. The constellations are Aquarius (The Water

An illustration from the 1800s shows the twelve signs of the zodiac.

Carrier), Pisces (The Fish), Aries (The Ram), Taurus (The Bull), Gemini (The Twins), Cancer (The Crab), Leo (The Lion), Virgo (The Maiden), Libra (The Scales), Scorpius, or Scorpio, (The Scorpion), Sagittarius (The Archer), and Capricorn (The Sea Goat). Most of the constellations are represented by animals, and the word *zodiac* comes from an ancient Greek word that means circle of animals.

The twelve zodiac constellations are thought to be among the oldest patterns in the sky that were recognized by early civilizations. Even Babylonian astronomers recognized these twelve constellations because the planets, the Sun, and the Moon seemed to travel through them during a year. And because those constellations were "touched" by the Sun, people thought they were much more important than any others.

There are many other constellations besides those in the zodiac, but those in the zodiac are probably best known because astrologers use them. In astrology, the zodiac signs are assigned to certain times of the year. Astrologers think that people born "under" certain zodiac signs (on certain dates) behave in different ways and have different characteristics.

FAMILIAR CONSTELLATIONS AND STARS

Early astronomers who charted the stars often connected them into shapes or designs. These shapes were then related to mythology, stories, animals, or other things of cultural importance. Many constellations and stars have common names that

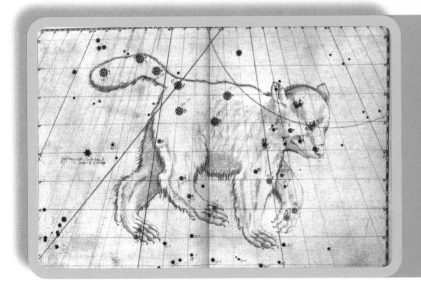

This illustration of Ursa Major was created by an astronomer who lived in the 1600s. Over the years, visibility of some of the stars has changed, causing many constellations to appear slightly different than they used to.

are familiar to many, such as Orion, Canis Major, and the Big and Little Dippers. But for other cultures, or time periods, constellations may be known by different names.

The Bears

Ursa Major, which means "Great Bear," and Ursa Minor, or "Little Bear," are a well-known constellations in the northern sky. Both constellations have the same general pattern—four stars make up a rectangular shape that represents the body. The heads and legs of the bears are made up of stars that are often too faint to see. Because only parts of the bears' bodies are bright enough to easily see, these two constellations are often called the Big and Little Dippers.

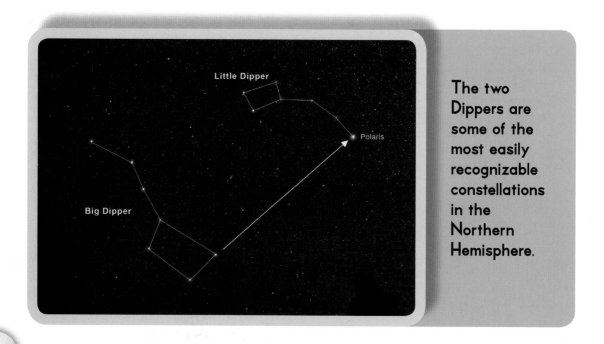

Little Dipper

Polaris

Big Dipper

The two Dippers are some of the most easily recognizable constellations in the Northern Hemisphere.

Pegasus

The ancient Greek myth of Pegasus the flying horse is responsible for the naming of several constellations that can be seen in the Northern Hemisphere in the summer. According to legends, a

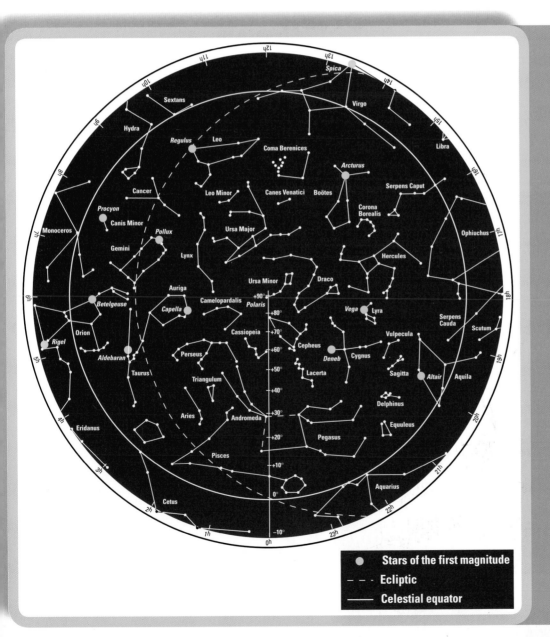

This star chart shows most of the major constellations in the northern celestial hemisphere.

Greek hero named Perseus rode Pegasus to save Andromeda from Cetus, the sea monster. Pegasus, Perseus, Andromeda, Cetus, and Andromeda's parents—Cassiopeia and Cepheus—are northern constellations.

Orion

People looking at the northern celestial hemisphere can see the Orion constellation from nearly everywhere on Earth. The stars' arrangement makes it appear as though a man—Orion—stands in the night sky with a bow and arrow and his club raised

The three stars in the center of this image make up Orion's belt. The pink dot below them is the Orion Nebula, which makes up part of his sword. Betelguese is the bright star in the upper left corner on Orion's shoulder. Rigel sits at Orion's foot, at the bottom right.

high. Three stars form Orion's belt, in a pattern that is easy to spot. (In fact, many people can identify the Orion constellation by looking for his three-star belt.) Such noticeable patterns are called **asterisms**. From left to right the stars in his belt are Alnitak, Alnilam, and Mintaka. The star Betelgeuse—sometimes known as Beetlejuice—is a red giant star, and sits on Orion's right shoulder. Rigel—the brightest star in the constellation—lies on Orion's left foot.

Orion is not alone in the skies. Two constellations represent his loyal hunting dogs. Canis Major—which includes Sirius, the brightest star in the sky—and Canis Minor, chase the other animal constellations around the sky, but never catch them. The Lepus constellation—the hare—can be seen hiding near Orion's feet.

The River

Eridanus, or The River constellation, starts at Orion's foot and flows south to its brightest star, Achernar. The constellation supposedly earned its name from a Greek myth about Phaeton. He kept asking his father, Helios the Sun god, to let him drive the chariot that Helios drove across the sky each day. Helios would not allow it because he worried that Phaeton was not strong enough to control the horses. Finally he gave in. Phaeton drove the chariot, but, in fact, could not control the horses. He drove all over the sky, up and down, freezing and then burning Earth.

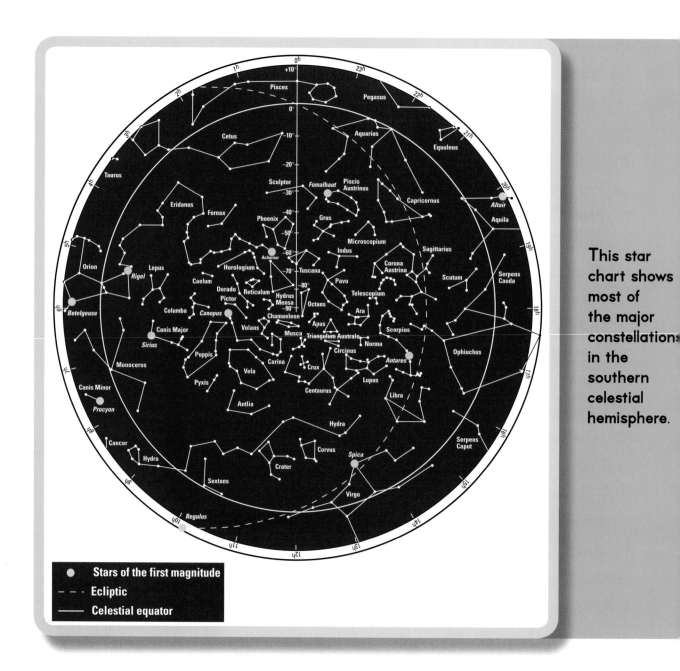

This star chart shows most of the major constellations in the southern celestial hemisphere.

Stars of the first magnitude
Ecliptic
Celestial equator

Zeus, king of the gods, was not happy when he saw how Phaeton was driving and threw a thunderbolt at him. Phaeton fell off the chariot and into the river. The River supposedly represents the path Phaeton took, and Achernar marks where he fell.

A STARGAZER'S GUIDE

Astronomers and scientists use special telescopes on Earth and on satellites or spacecraft in space. This specialized equipment allows them to see details and collect other types of data that teaches them more about stars and celestial objects. But you do not have to be a professional astronomer to marvel at the starry night sky.

Observatories and planetariums are good places to learn about and view the stars. Some observatories have special programs for times when specific constellations or celestial bodies are visible. Many of these places also have strong telescopes that they allow the public to use to view the sky.

Stargazing on your own can be as simple as looking up at the sky at night. An up-to-date star map can help identify the stars you may see in the sky. Study the map and become familiar with the patterns of one or two constellations. That way you will know what to look for when you gaze at the night sky. You might even consider getting a planisphere. This a circular device—often made of plastic or very stiff paper—that has two discs, one on top of the other. The discs are fastened together, but can still rotate. The bottom disc has a chart of the stars, while the top has dates and times. To use the planisphere, turn the discs until they are aligned for a specific date and time. The chart will show you which celestial objects you may be able to see. Planispheres can be found at many bookstores or science stores.

Many stars are bright enough to see with the unaided, or naked, eye. But to get more detail, you might consider using binoculars or a telescope. Some experts say that you would not need a very strong telescope to see basic constellations and some other celestial objects. However, you should NEVER look

The Pleiades, which are also known as the Seven Sisters, is a cluster of stars that can be seen without a telescope. Part of the Taurus constellation, this star cluster is made of hundreds of stars.

directly at the Sun or use regular telescopes or binoculars to look at it. If you look directly at it, the Sun's rays can do serious damage to your eyes. Special equipment is made to view the Sun safely.

Whether you use a telescope, binoculars, or just your eyes, you must choose your stargazing location carefully. The best way to view stars is when the sky is cloudless and very dark, with little or no light pollution. Light pollution is the light from city lights, headlights, or other human-made objects that can obscure your view of the night sky. Because it will be nighttime, the dark place you choose should be safe, and you should have an adult or older family member with you. Be prepared to spend a while stargazing, because it can take thirty minutes for your eyes to adjust to the dark. You might not be able to find the constellations you are looking for on your first try. But careful observations and patience will eventually pay off, and you will see the twinkling lights of stars that are light-years away.

THE CLOSEST STARS

Here are some of the stars that are the closest to Earth.

CLOSEST STARS	DISTANCE FROM EARTH (LIGHT-YEARS)	VISUAL MAGNITUDE	CONSTELLATION IN WHICH STAR IS FOUND
The Sun	0.00001585 (93 million miles or 150 million km)	-26.72	
Proxima Centauri	4.24	11.05	Centaurus
Rigel Centauri A	4.36	0.00	Orion
Centauri B	4.36	1.34	Centaurus
Barnard's Star	5.9	9.53	Ophiuchus
Wolf 359	7.8	13.44	Leo
Lalande 21185	8.3	7.47	Ursa Major
Sirius A	8.58	-1.43	Canis Major
Sirius B	8.58	8.44	Canis Major
UV Ceti A	8.7	12.54	Cetus
UV Ceti B	8.7	12.99	Cetus

THE BRIGHTEST STARS

Here are some of the brightest stars that can be seen from Earth.

BRIGHTEST STARS	DISTANCE FROM EARTH (LIGHT-YEARS)	VISUAL MAGNITUDE	CONSTELLATION
Sirius	8.6	-1.44	Canis Major
Canopus	313	-0.72	Carina
Arcturus	37	-0.05	Boötes
Alpha Centauri	4.35	0.01	Centaurus
Vega	25.3	0.03	Lyra
Capella	42.2	0.08	Auriga
Rigel	773	0.18	Orion
Procyon	11.41	0.34	Canis Minor
Achernar	144	0.50	Eridanus
Betelgeuse	640	0.30-1.00 (varies)	Orion

GLOSSARY

asterism—A small group of stars that form a pattern, often within another constellation. The Big Dipper, part of the Great Bear constellation, is an asterism.

astronomer—A person who studies objects in space.

atom—The tiniest particle of an element. Atoms cannot be divided.

celestial—Having to do with the sky or space.

constellation—A collection of stars.

gravity—The force that causes objects to be attracted to one another. Gravitational force increases as objects are closer together or for objects with more mass.

interstellar space—The space between the stars, which scientists call the interstellar medium. It is not really empty space, but filled with clouds of different gases—mostly hydrogen—and tiny solid particles.

light-year—A unit of measurement used to measure distances in space. One light-year is equivalent to 5.89 trillion miles (9.46 trillion km).

luminosity—The rate at which a star radiates light energy. Stars can be described and classified based on their luminosity.

magnitude—A unit of measure in a star luminosity scale. The brightest stars are of the first magnitude. The faintest stars are of the sixth magnitude.

molecule—A small part of a substance that has all its properties and is made up of one or more atoms.

plasma—A substance similar to gas, but containing positively charged particles called ions and negatively charged electrons. Plasma is considered the fourth state of matter, after solids, liquids, and gases.

singularity—The end-stage of a dying star, or matter falling into a black hole.

FIND OUT MORE

BOOKS

Driscoll, Michael. *A Child's Introduction to the Night Sky: The Story of the Stars, Planets, and Constellations—and How You Can Find Them in the Sky.* New York: Black Dog and Leventhal, 2004.

Scagell, Robin, and Jacqueline Mitton. *Night Sky Atlas.* New York: DK Publishing, 2007.

Simon, Seymour. *Stars.* New York: HarperCollins, 2006.

Stott, Carole. *Space Exploration.* New York: DK Publishing, 2004.

WEBSITES

Curious about Astronomy? Ask an Astronomer
http://curious.astro.cornell.edu

HubbleSite
http://hubblesite.org

NASA Home Page
www.nasa.gov/home/index.html

NASA Kids' Club
http://www.nasa.gov/audience/forkids/kidsclub/flash/index.html

NASA Star Count: Student Observation Network
www.nasa.gov/audience/foreducators/son/energy/starcount/index.html

Space.com: Live television from NASA
www.space.com/

Voyager: The Interstellar Mission
http://voyager.jpl.nasa.gov

BIBLIOGRAPHY

The author found these resources especially helpful while researching this book.

Aguilar, David A. *Planets, Stars, and Galaxies.* Washington, D.C.: National Geographic Society, 2007.

Baumann, Mary K., Will Hopkins, Loralee Nolletti, and Michael Soluri. *Cosmos: Images from Here to the Edge of the Universe.* London: Duncan Baird Publishers Ltd., 2007.

Dickinson, Terence. *NightWatch: A Practical Guide to Viewing the Universe.* Buffalo, NY: Firefly Books, 2006.

Hewitt-White, Ken. *Patterns in the Sky: An Introduction to Stargazing.* Night Sky. Astronomy for Everyone. Cambridge, MA: New Track Media. Sky Publishing, 2006.

Kerrod, Robin. *The Stargazer's Guide to the Universe: A Complete Visual Guide to Interpreting the Cosmos.* Barron's Educational Series, Inc. London: Quarto Publishing plc, 2005.

Moore, Patrick. *Firefly Guide to Stars and Planets.* new ed. Buffalo, NY: Firefly Books Ltd. 2005.

Price, Pat. *The Backyard Stargazer: An Absolute Beginner's Guide to Skywatching with and without a Telescope.* Gloucester, MA: Quarry Books, 2005.

Ridpath, Ian. *Stars and Planets.* Smithsonian Handbooks. London: Dorling Kindersley Ltd., 2002.

INDEX

Page numbers in **boldface** indicate photos or illustrations.

THE STARS

ABOUT THE AUTHOR

Gail Mack is a freelance writer and editor. She is the author of several books for students and also writes poetry. She began her career as a reporter for the *Boston Herald Traveler*, where she covered metropolitan news and education. Ms. Mack later worked as a reporter and editor for the *New York Herald Tribune*, *The New York Times*, and other daily and weekly newspapers in the New York metropolitan area. She is a Sagittarius.